Healing Brokenness

Healing Brokenness Through Creativity and Play

A Practical Guide to Pastoral Care in Times of Crises

Dr. Carolyn V. Hodge

I AM The Living Word Ministries, Inc.
Bowie, Maryland

Healing Brokenness Through Creativity and Play
Copyright © 2017 by I AM The Living Word Ministries, Inc.

Scripture quotations in this book are taken from the King James Version of the Bible, unless otherwise noted in the text. Scripture quotations marked AMP are taken from the Amplified Version of the Bible. Scripture quotations marked NIV are taken from the New International Version of the Bible. The following Bible translation was used: The Comparative Study Bible, copyright ©1984 by The Zondervan Bible Publishers.

All rights reserved under International Copyright Law. No part of this book may be reproduced or transmitted in any form or by any means without written permission of the Publisher, except for the inclusion of brief quotations in a review.

Cover design by TLH Designs, www.tlhdesigns.com
Book layout and design by Kingdom Living Publishing,
    www.kingdomlivingbooks.com

For information about this book or to contact the author, write to:

I AM The Living Word Ministries, Inc.
3450 Crain Highway, Suite 231
Bowie, Maryland 20716

Published by:

I AM The Living Word Ministries, Inc.
3450 Crain Highway, Suite 231
Bowie, Maryland 20716

Published in the United States of America.

ISBN 978-0-692-71954-1

Contents

1. Introduction — 7

2. What the Scriptures Say About Creativity and Play — 19

3. Creativity and Play: Philosophical And Scholarly View — 25

4. Ministering to People Through Creativity And Play — 41

5. Conclusion — 53

Chapter 1

Introduction

As individuals go through periods of difficulty in their lives, they often wonder how they will survive during those hard times, especially during times of what one calls crises. A crisis could be the result of losing a loved one as a result of death or losing a loved one as a result of divorce. In addition, the crises could be the result of an onset of a major illness with debilitating physical and emotional conditions. The outcome of such an illness could be the inability to be mobile—the need to rely on walkers or wheelchairs. The outcome of such an illness could ultimately be death. The crises could be the result of dreams unfulfilled or the loss of a job, or the loss concerning an opportunity for career progression that has become unrealized. Regardless of the type of loss, the individual may see such a loss as a crisis for his/her life. The resulting loss may cause individuals to have feelings of dismay, feelings of confusion, feelings of being destitute, feelings of being at one's wits end, and feelings about whether or not they will survive the trauma of the loss. At such times, the person may feel hurt. Some of these hurts may be physical, psychological, or spiritual or a combination of two or more of these entities. As ministers, we need to seek effective ways of intervention during such times for our parishioners. As ministers with the responsibility for administering healing and wholeness, we will need to seek creative ways to be more effective as we minister to the individual and/or to their family members during such times of crises. As ministers, we should begin to consider the role of creativity and play as potential means to healing and wholeness.

In the book, _Healing in the Midst of Brokenness_, we explored and considered the depth of meaning associated with healing and wholeness. We discovered that healing and wholeness may not mean, necessarily, a cure, but a healing that takes place through the

Introduction

acceptance of the present condition and despite the present condition, one finds a sense of peace—healing and wholeness—peace of mind and peace of the spirit. This book will present and explore creativity and play as useful means to providing healing and wholeness during times of crises.

This book will begin this process by taking a look at creativity and play as presented in some of the passages of the Bible, by looking at creativity and play as documented by philosophical thinkers, by assessing the theological implications on the topics of creativity and play, and by presenting some ways of engaging those going through crises in creativity and play with the goal of administering healing and wholeness. By presenting multiple ways of ministering to people who are experiencing very traumatic and difficult times, it is the author's hope that some of these ways will be effective in ministry and used to meet the needs of people.

As a backdrop to this effort, I will be sharing some personal and ministerial experiences that I have encountered. Greater details of these accounts will be presented herewith were not shared in the initial book. It is my hope that my personal experiences will assist ministers with practical and real-life experiences to help you to minister more effectively to meet the needs of your parishioners.

My mother was diagnosed with breast cancer at the age of 69. After a lumpectomy, radiation, and chemotherapy, the disease went into remission. Five years later, it was discovered that the disease had returned and was attacking her vital organs—the lungs and the digestive system. In observing my mother as she experienced this trauma in her life, I noticed that she did not appear to have any melancholy feelings about her condition. She seemed to have had an incredible sense of peace during an extremely critical time in her life.

Mom had always professed her faith as a Christian. In the early stages of her life, she grew up and attended an AME Zion Church in Rock Hill, S.C. I am told that she would race her cousin to the church and she would always end up on the front row of the church. During these early years, she lived with her grandparents, who were sharecroppers. Although they were poor by today's standards, they were rich in their faith. They passed their faith in God on to their children and grandchildren.

Introduction

At the age of fifteen, she moved to Durham, N.C., to live with her mother, who had traveled to North Carolina to find employment. She continued in her church tradition by attending church services and fully participating in a myriad of church activities. Mom was grounded fully in her faith and in her religious tradition. I believe that it is this grounding—her faith and trust in God—that served as her benchmark for healing and wholeness regardless of her physical condition.

There was something else that I observed about Mom during this time. At age 69, Mom began to take singing lessons and she began to travel extensively. Mom always enjoyed traveling—going and experiencing new places. She and my Dad had traveled throughout the country and had traveled to the Caribbean. So, I was not surprised that she had started to travel, but I was surprised that she had started taking voice lessons. She was a faithful student and seemed to enjoy the lessons immensely.

Some years after her death, I began to discover that Mom had found creative ways for dealing with her illness. I believe that her faith bolstered her during this crisis. I believe, further, that the travel and the singing lessons served as "play" for her during a time of physical and emotional suffering. Mom was being healed and experiencing wholeness through creativity and play.

A young woman had experienced heart-breaking trauma as a result of spousal separation and divorce. She had grown up in a family that nurtured and cared for one another. Her parents and her two sets of grandparents were examples of loving, caring, and successful marriages and families. This is not to say that everything was always perfect within the marriages. It merely shows that the spouses worked at their marriages—showed compassion and understanding towards one another—and managed to overcome obstacles and difficult situations in their marriages.

By the time this woman was married, her family history had reflected the following. Her mom and dad had been married thirty-one years. Her maternal grandparents had been married for fifty-two years and her paternal grandparents had been married for forty-one years. The only thing that had separated the spouses was death. Thus, this woman had an expectation that she

Introduction

would have a successful marriage. Success to her was that the marriage would survive—a marriage based on trust, understanding, and love. For her, this would not be the case. Within two years of the marriage, she had to call the police to get her husband out of the house. He was threatening violence, something that he had done several times before. At this juncture, the violence was escalating beyond verbal abuse to the point of physical altercations.

The young woman found it very difficult to sort through her feelings. Quite often, just prior to the incident I mentioned above, she was reluctant to go home, because she did not know what kind of mood her spouse would be in. She stated that she was afraid to go home. This was trauma for her—emotional trauma, psychological trauma. She was not sure how she could cope with the situation. Shortly, after her spouse was removed from the home and after the court had sanctioned the removal, she appeared to be mentally exhausted. She opted to seek counseling to assist her through this difficulty. Initially, she sought counseling from the pastor at her church. She was told that as a wife, the husband is the head of the household. Further, she was told that she was to submit to her husband. This counseling left her confused and angry. It appeared to her that her pastor was uncaring about her as a person. He was only espousing biblical Scriptures, but not truly looking at the situation—the hurt that she was experiencing, the sense of loss that she was experiencing. The pastor did not counsel her spouse, nor did the pastor paraphrase any Scripture pertaining to his behavior toward his wife. As a minimum, perhaps the pastor should have mentioned verse 25 of that same passage in Ephesians 5, which states, *"Husbands, love your wives, even as Christ also loved the church, and gave Himself for it …"* Further, the pastor did not assert the passage in the Scriptures that focuses on God's disdain for men who mistreat their wives. This Scripture states, *"… take heed to your spirit, and let none deal treacherously against the wife of his youth."* Further, another Scripture that could have caused her spouse to have a change of heart toward her is God hates *"… him who covers his garment [his wife] with violence"* (AMP).

She had attended multiple counseling sessions with her pastor. Her spouse attended some of them. Not once did she hear anything that would cause her spouse to have ownership for what had happened in their marriage. Later, her spouse told her that he had told the pastor in a one-on-one session with him that their marital situation was not that bad. He went on to say to her that his parents had been through much worse in their marriage. Clearly, his parents would not have been considered ideal role models.

She was horrified at the thought that her situation could progress to even greater violence. She found it difficult to process the thought that she would have to live her marital life in violence and uncertainty—never knowing what to expect when she arrived home from work, church, and/or visiting with her family or friends. She felt alone. She felt betrayed. She had wished that she had not ever brought the matter to the pastor's attention.

After receiving some suggestions from the county spousal abuse council, she contacted a Christian Psychologist. This individual provided her with the guidance that she needed to work through the trauma of a broken marriage. The Psychologist helped her to mitigate the experiences through reflection questions—getting the young woman to see that she did not over react to her marital situation and that she had taken the most appropriate course of action to solve her dilemma. Further, the Psychologist informed her that the Bible did not mean for wives to remain in abusive marriages. She reminded her about the role and responsibility, biblically speaking, the husband was to have toward his wife—to love her as Christ loves the church (paraphrased). Christ reveals gentleness and compassion toward the church. She was told that husbands were to do the same—deal gently and compassionately toward the wife.

In addition to the trauma that the woman experienced as she dealt with these events and circumstances in her life, I noticed that she began to direct her attention to other things. She had mentioned to me that her Psychologist had suggested that she needed to refocus her attention on positive things. To hash and rehash the traumatic events was not leading her toward healing and wholeness. Thus, she began to refocus her attention on the doctoral thesis that she was developing in the field of Electrical Engineering. In addition, she began to participate in the weekly prayer service on Fridays at her church. (She became a member of a new church, which was located closer to her home.)

Further, she began to go to musicals, Broadway plays, and concerts; and she embarked upon several cruises to Europe and the Middle East. Her doctoral degree allowed her to travel to Australia, Singapore, and many other lands as a part of her professional endeavors. In short, she started doing fun things for herself. She had discovered Healing through Creativity and Play through her career and other outside interests. She was becoming with each new adventure a "new creation" in Christ.

This young woman was creating something new in her professional field. Both on the job and in school, she was creating that which had not existed before. This was fun to her. She was at play in school and at work. In addition, she was experiencing play as she experienced recreational activities outside of the workplace. These new endeavors caused her to laugh and enjoy life more fully. As she traveled to new and interesting places and experienced different things, she was discovering that there is a much larger world that is filled with the joys of our Creator. She was healing and receiving wholeness through creating new adventures for her life. All of which were pleasurable and fun.

Chapter 2

What the Scriptures Say About Creativity and Play

On the Matter of Creativity

"In the beginning God created ..." (Genesis 1:1).

From the very beginning, as we read in the Scriptures, God is about the business of creativity. In the Scriptures, we see God actively creating:

"Let there be light ... Let there be a firmament ... Heaven (and) ... Seas ... let the dry land appear ... Earth ... and God saw that it was good" (Genesis 1:3-10).

Further reading reveals that God is actively creating everything associated with God's new creation, including the birds, fish, grass, herbs, fruit trees, and a host of other things associated therewith. God does not stop creating here. God goes on to create human existence: *"Let us make man in our image, in our likeness, and let them rule over the fish of the sea and the birds of the air, over the livestock, over all the earth, and over all the creatures that move along the ground"* (Genesis 1:26). God goes on to tell the humans in verse 28 (NIV) to *"Be fruitful and increase in number; fill the earth and subdue it. Rule over the fish of the sea and the birds of the air and over every living creature that moves on the ground."* God classifies God's creativity as "very good."

God is actively engaged in creativity. Not only is God actively engaged in it, God tells the humans to be actively engaged in creativity. God tells them to have "dominion" over God's creativity. The word "dominion" is derived from the Hebrew word, "radah," which means to "tread down; i.e., subjugate ... prevail against, reign, rule ... rule over, take."[1] The humans are to "Be fruitful

What the Scriptures Say about Creativity and Play

and increase in number ... to fill the earth and subdue it. To subdue comes from the Hebrew word, "kabash." This word means to conquer, to subjugate, or to bring into subjection.[2] In order to have dominion over God's creativity, one must be creative. God tells us in Scripture that we, humans, are created in the image of God. To be created in God's image ... God's character ... God's self ..., we should have the character of God. We are told that we are created in God's "likeness." To be created in God's "likeness" means in the Hebrew ("de-muwth") similitude, to "resemble" God, to "model" God, and to operate in the "same manner" to God.[3] According to the Webster's Dictionary, similitude refers to being a "counterpart" a "double," a "correspondence in kind or quality."[4] Thus, humankind has been created by God to be a counterpart in God's creativity. We are created in God's likeness to be creative. We should have the character of God and we should resemble God and we should be creative. We should be like God. God created the heavens and earth. God continues to create through us. We create through God. In order to be fruitful and increase, one must be creative. To subdue that which has been created requires one to be creative.

Another way of looking at creativity is being at "play." As God created the heavens and the earth, God's response was, "... *it was very good*" (Genesis 1:31). It sounds like God was having fun at being creative. God was at play. God calls us, likewise, to be at play—to be creative—to have some enthusiasm and anticipation about what we do while we aspire to reach "dominion" over the things that God has set at our hands to do. We are called to be creative. We are called to play.

I learned in my secular work life that I enjoyed creating new policies, programs, and events associated with the Civil Rights Program. The challenge of performing my job was assuring that the policies were approved and authorized by the Head of the Federal agency for which I worked. Meeting the challenge head on and seeing the task to completion was fun for me. I was at play while being creative. I enjoyed the results of the finished products. Upon retirement, I felt that I was among many who had a hand at creating a new society within the United States—a society that welcomes diversity and

What the Scriptures Say about Creativity and Play

inclusion of multi-ethnic peoples. I believe that I was at work—at play—with God, creating a whole new world.

On the Matter of Play

Concerning "play," the Bible states the following:

> *"And David said unto Michal, It was before the Lord, which chose me before thy father, and before all his house, to appoint me ruler over the people of the Lord, over Israel: therefore will I play before the Lord"* (2 Samuel 6:21).

This passage is from the story of King David. The Ark of the Covenant was being returned to Jerusalem, after it had been stolen out of the city and had remained for a season in the house of Obed-edom, the Gitite. As David and his men were bringing back the ark into the city, the Scriptures stated that "David danced before the Lord with all his might ..." The background of the Scripture tells us that David danced so hard—with all his might—that he literally danced out of his outer clothing. David was chided by his wife, Michal, for making a spectacle of himself, from her point of view. Michal was the daughter of Saul, the former King. David responded to Michal, *"It was before the Lord, who chose me rather than your father or anyone from his house when He appointed me ruler over the Lord's people Israel* (NIV); **therefore will I play before the Lord."** (bold emphasis added) The NIV version of the bolded statement translates the word "play" into "celebrate." The Amplified version of this same passage reads, *"Therefore will I* **make merry (in pure enjoyment)** *(bold added) before the Lord."* Play in Hebrew ("sachaq") means to make merry, to laugh in pleasure and detraction, and/or to rejoice. King David was exceedingly happy about the return of the Ark of the Covenant, because the ark represented the very Presence of God. Wherever the ark was the blessings of God flourished. So, King David was rejoicing before the Lord in dance and making merry. David was at play before the Lord.

Chapter 3

Creativity and Play: Philosophical and Scholarly View

Creativity Defined and Examined

Creativity is viewed by Mihaly Csikszentmihalyi "as a process that unfolds over a lifetime ..."[1] This scholar believes that creativity "arises from the synergy of many sources ... not only from the mind of a single person."[2] He says that "a genuinely creative accomplishment is almost never the result of a sudden insight, ... but comes after years of hard work."[3] He goes on to say that "creativity results from the interaction of a system composed of three elements: a culture that contains symbolic rules, a person who brings novelty into the symbolic domain, and a field of experts who recognize and validate the innovative. All three are necessary for a creative idea, product or discovery to take place."[4] He defines creativity as "a process by which a symbolic domain in culture is changed."[5] He goes on to say that, "Creativity can be observed only in the interrelations of a system made up of three main parts." One part is the domain, "which consists of a set of symbolic rules and procedures."[6] An example that he cites for domain is Mathematics. "The second component of creativity is the field, which includes all the individuals who act as gatekeepers to the domain."[7] It is the job of the gatekeepers to determine whether or not a new product or a new idea "should be included in the domain."[8] The "third component of the creative system is the individual person.

Creativity occurs when a person, using the symbols of a given domain such as music, engineering, business, or mathematics, has a new idea or sees a new pattern, and when this novelty is selected by the appropriate field for inclusion into the relevant domain."[9] From this perspective, the writer sees creativity as "any act, idea, or product that changes an existing domain, or that transforms an existing domain into a new one."[10] Thus, a creative person is viewed as one "whose thoughts and actions change a domain, or establish a new domain."[11] Keep in mind, however, that without the explicit or implicit consent of the responsible field, the domain cannot be changed.

The creative person may experience some frustrations, particularly if his/her ideas are not readily accepted by the domain or the field. Sometimes whole segments of society are left out of the opportunity to reach their "potential for excellence."[12] John W. Gardner, former Secretary of Health, Education, and Welfare, saw the potential for excellence as a birthright of every person. The riots of the 1960s appeared to confirm Gardner's position. The riots were the result of segments of society that had been historically denied access to the mainstream of America. They had been denied their opportunity to reach their full potential for excellence. Thus, they had begun to revolt. My secular position, Director of Equal Employment Opportunity (EEO), was to ensure equal access of opportunity to minorities and women, the disabled, and individuals over the age of 60 within the Federal agencies for which I worked. This, indeed, was a "voluntary movement" that would "inform people of their options and then help them find their voices and their power in the political process."[13] This was my job as an EEO official within the Federal government—to ensure opportunities for career advancement were in place, to ensure that employees had a venue to raise any points of contention, and to provide counseling to assuage potential problems between management and employees. In other words, I was responsible for ensuring that Federal employees reached their "potential for excellence."[14] This was an area of creativity. An area where the domain—the political process—accepted, under law, and voluntarily approves and agrees to the opportunity for equality of access. This is an area where the field—voting rights and equal opportunity in employment, housing, and education—under law and voluntarily, complied. The newly formed social order created opportunities for access of myriad members of society to reach their full potential for excellence. Many of whom I came in contact with over the years had what is termed "emotional intelligence ... which includes ... zeal and persistence, and the ability to motivate oneself" to reach their full potential.[15]

As a result of the laws that were passed in the 1960s, many began to assert themselves, to redirect their life's goals and objectives, and work toward achieving their lifelong dreams—their potential for excellence. Goleman says, "Our passions, when well exercised, have wisdom; they guide our thinking, our values, our survival."[16] The passions of the disenfranchised guided their abilities to reach their potential for excellence.

Goleman also noted that "anxiety undermines the intellect ... The anxious are more likely to fail even given superior scores on intelligence tests ..."[17] When a person experiences anxiety about a task, an error is likely to occur. Quite often the anxious person is saying to him/herself, "I won't be able to do this" or "I'm just no good at this kind of test."[18] By the same token, some people are adept at harnessing their anxiety; thereby causing them to prepare, for example, more thoroughly for an upcoming test or examination.

As ministers, I believe our task is to foster inclusiveness within the church, the body of Christ. We are to encourage members of our congregations to reach their full potential, to harness their emotions and anxiety, to plan for and where possible, to anticipate some of the challenges of life. We can encourage them to meet the challenges in creative ways. I believe we are to give them something to hope for. Hope, according to Goleman, "does more than offer a bit of solace amid affliction; it plays a surprisingly potent role in life, offering an advantage in realms as diverse as school achievement and bearing up in onerous jobs."[19] Hope is stated by C. R. Snyder, the University of Kansas psychologist, as "believing you have both the will and the way to accomplish your goals, whatever they may be."[20] The adage of "Hope Springs Eternal" plays out. From the emotional intelligence perspective, "having hope means that one will not give in to overwhelming anxiety, a defeatist attitude, or depression in the face of difficult challenges or setbacks. People, who are hopeful, experience less depression than those who are without hope. They are able to "maneuver through life in pursuit of their goals, are less anxious in general, and have fewer emotional distresses."[21] Thus, our task as ministers is to offer hope and optimism—"that things will turn out all right in life, despite setbacks and frustrations."[22] How do we do this? Let us make certain that we provide our parishioners with sources and human resources that have the expertise in their chosen fields—people who can direct them towards accomplishing their life dreams and goals.

Earlier I spoke about the difficulties that a young woman had experienced with her spouse. Prior to the occurrence of violence, she found herself to be a victim of criticism. As far as her spouse was concerned, she could do nothing right and nothing that she did was good, not even the meals.

For many years prior to marriage she had become an outstanding cook—a connoisseur of fine foods. She and her Dad would challenge each other in the kitchen as to which one could prepare the best possible meal. As a result, she developed into a gifted and creative cook. The family raved about her cooking. She was into the "presentation" of the meal—the colors as well as the taste had to be just right. Yet, her spouse never complimented her on her cooking. She would often probe him for a response about the food. At best, he would come up with, "Aw, it's alright." For the most part, he would be critical of what she had prepared. The worst way to motivate someone is through negative criticism.[23] "Criticisms are voiced as personal attacks rather than complaints that can be acted upon..."[24] This young woman was criticized, yet never offered any feedback as to how she could improve the situation. She was left in the dark. She had no idea of how she stood with her spouse. She felt unloved and unappreciated. Negative criticism offers no means for taking corrective action. The person experiencing negative criticism is left to figure out on his/her own what next steps should be taken to rectify the situation. Positive criticism provides feedback about how the situation or set of issues or circumstances can be improved. The recipient of this type of criticism has a lighted path to take toward making positive change.

If the need arises where one needs to critique a situation, one needs to focus on the situation and/or circumstances, not the person. The critique should be specific about what may have gone wrong, what needs to change, and how one might consider proceeding.

Harry Levinson, a psychoanalyst, notes that it is very important to praise—find something to talk about that is positive concerning the situation. Levinson tells us to offer solutions—"suggestions about how to take care of [the] problems."[25] Levinson goes on to tell us that one should be present when giving critiques—leaving written notes and memoranda are not good ways for dealing with critiques. In each instance, be certain to be sensitive and have empathy for the individual. Consider how you would feel if you were receiving such a critique. Try to end the critique with positive comments.

The individual receiving a critique has responsibility for how they receive the critique. The individual needs to assess him/herself to assure that he/she is not responding defensively instead of being responsible for his/her actions. The individual must learn to see the value in the information and not see the critique as "a personal attack."[26] If the critique proves to be too upsetting, then one should request that they resume their discussion at a later time. This will allow time for cooling down and time to better digest the information. Both parties should try to see the critique as an opportunity to work better together and to solve problems. They should see that this is not "an adversarial situation."[27]

Because of her difficulties with her spouse, the young woman had become very angry. With the help of counseling from the Psychologist, she found creative ways for diffusing her anger. As ministers, who may be called upon to mediate situations like hers, we will need to develop some skills. "A key social ability is empathy, understanding others' feelings and taking their perspective, and respecting differences in how people feel about things."[28] We must learn to be good listeners and question-askers. We must be able to distinguish between "what someone says or does" and "our own reactions and judgments ..."[29] Our task should be to aid the person in finding solutions to their situation or to assist them with coping skills as a process through difficult times. We may even need to take some training to develop and/or refine "the arts of cooperation, conflict resolution, and negotiating compromise."[30]

Play Defined and Examined

Catherine Garvey presents play as "a period of dramatically expanding knowledge of self, the physical and social world, and systems of communication ..."[31] "Karl Groos, a philosopher, saw in the play-fighting of animals and the imitative behavior of children a preparation for adult performance."[32] G. Stanley Hall, a psychologist, noted that playful behavior changes with age. His theory of recapitulation maintains that "the play of children reflects the course of evolution from prehistoric hominids to the present. The history of the race is recapitulated in each child's development."[33] Both of these theories were influenced by Darwinism. Exuberance is a relatively "universal characteristic of much playful behavior. The young of higher species frolic, frisk, gallop, gambol, cavort, and engage in mock combat, with every sign of pleasure and high spirits and with no apparent utilitarian objective. Such activities are suggested by Herbert Spencer, psychologist, as an expenditure of surplus energy.[34] These theories of play or playfulness (instinctive preparation, recapitulation, and surplus energy) have been either "discarded or revised and adapted to more current theoretical positions..."[35]

Garvey states that the following characteristics of play are critical to the definition of play. Garvey goes on to say that many "would accept the following inventory:

1. Play is pleasurable, enjoyable. Even when not actually accompanied by signs of mirth, it is still positively valued by the player.

2. Play has no extrinsic goals. Its motivations are intrinsic and serve no other objectives. In fact, it is more an enjoyment of means than an effort devoted to some particular end. In utilitarian terms, it is inherently unproductive.

3. Play is spontaneous and voluntary. It is not obligatory but is freely chosen by the player.

4. Play involves some active engagement on the part of the player.

Creativity and Play: Philosophical and Scholarly View

Each of these characteristics is partially typical of state other than play."[36] Work, sports, artistic endeavors, and lounging are all pleasurable. Lounging, however, does not engage others. Yet each of these could fit the definition of play, particularly, if one gets pleasure out of them.

"Play has been lined with creativity, problem-solving, language learning, the development of social roles, and a number of other cognitive and social phenomena."[37] It is interesting to note that as one observes children engaged at playing "make believe," they are engaged at play, but at the same time, they are mimicking the adults and behaviors that they have observed in the world around them. Thus, it appears that play is creative and a way of understanding the world around you. It appears to be a process toward maturation.[38] It is transformative. The players act out certain roles. Sometimes during the transformation process, their voices will change and their posture will change. If, for example, they are playing house, the boy will act out the role of the father, while the girl will act out the role of the mother. If one child is pretending to be a baby, then perhaps they will whine or whimper in order to get their way. Thusly, play is learned in the early stages of life. It is a process of transformation.

Role-play and "engaging in make-believe appear to contribute to the flexibility with which a child approaches situations and tasks."[39] Brian Sutton-Smith has suggested that play may heighten the ease with which new approaches or ideas can be adopted toward diverse materials.[40] "The imaginative pretender has the experience of manipulating, recombining, and extending associations between words and things, and between things, persons, and actions."[41] Thus, it appears that a child, engaged in make-believe, facilitates his/her development, including abstract thought. Play becomes a creative way of defining and discovering one's world.

Dr. Michael Koppel defines play as "a means of cooperative and collaborative engagement within self and between self and others that seek to heighten enjoyment of life experience by make space for the innovative within structured patterns of behavior. Play allows for making mistakes in attempts to move beyond the conventional in pursuit of the novel."[42] Koppel goes on to tell us that "ministers can provide care to misfit communities and care in the midst of transitional times." He defines misfits as "person, qualities, and experiences that do not correspond to dominant cultural paradigms or perspectives."[43]

Theological Implications of Creativity and Play

Quite often we, as ministers, view our role as "matters of preaching, teaching, administration of the sacraments, corporate worship, and pastoral care to the sick, hurting," and the marginalized.[44] Yet it is so much more, including what Koppel calls "misfit practices."[45] Such practices, according to Koppel's definition of "misfit practices," might include some of the following: "church dinners, bazaars, actions, ice cream socials," and a host of other sundry social activities and events. This provides an opportunity for the members of the congregation to play. "Jurgen Moltmann calls [this] 'purpose-free fellowship' of the church."[46] Social events such as these provide opportunities for the members of the congregation to fellowship with one another and to meet new people, who may be attracted to the events. Such events serve as a means to reach out to the community to present the Spirit of Christ through social engagements. These are opportunities to "meet family members and neighbors who otherwise would not have entered the church building."[47] Winnicott calls such encounters "potential space" ... the area where congregation and community members gather to form relationships."[48] Thus, social events, places of play, "provide a space" where pastoral care giving may occur.[49]

Chapter 4

Ministering to People Through Creativity and Play

Ministering to people suffering from the ravages of cancer, such as my Mom, and ministering to people suffering from the hardships and grief associated with divorce, such as the young woman we discussed earlier, may be challenging to ministers. However, based upon what I have learned as a result of researching and presenting this Chapter, ministering to the suffering is a matter of approach and a matter of embracing creativity and play as vital entities for engaging the suffering—those who are in need of healing and wholeness from their brokenness. We need to help them to get into what is termed the "flow." Flow is that "quality of experience" one feels when one is "involved with (an) activity." The flow allows for the impetus to continue the activity, because "things (are) going well as an almost automatic, effortless, yet highly focused state of consciousness." (Csikszentmihalyi, 110).

Social events, outside of the "norm" of "important ministry" (administering the sacraments, preaching and teaching the Scriptures, and ministering to the sick and shut-in) are vital to ministering to the needs of the body of Christ, the church. As we minister healing and wholeness we can utilize our skills of empathy, attentive listening, asking questions, and providing one-on-one time. In doing so we provide the opportunity to better know our individual parishioners—to share in their daily lives, including the ups and the downs, to share in their grief, and to share in their sense of being stranded in their grief, illness, despair, aloneness, and/or guilt. The word stranded is defined by Webster as being run, driven, or caused to drift. Further, to strand means "to leave in a strange or an unfavorable place especially without funds or means to depart." For many this feeling of being stranded is like being in a strange place spiritually and mentally—without the means to depart from it. This is where ministers can begin to be effective in ministering to those who are dealing with grief and a sense of being stranded.

William L. Self tells us in this book, <u>Survival Kit for the Stranded</u>, that "the church ought to be a place where people can come together and grieve."[1] Too often, we mask our sense of being stranded by covering ourselves with things, such as fine cars, homes with manicured lawns, and association memberships. Sometimes our sense of being stranded—a sense of aloneness without any help or hope—leads to addictive behaviors, such as alcoholism, drug abuse, overeating and a host of other things. Thus, the church should be a place where individuals may come and share their concerns—their sense of being stranded. A Spanish philosopher, Unamuno, observed, "The proper use of a Temple is to provide a place where people can grieve together."[2]

Grief is a universal experience. Grief is suffering caused by a sense of loss—loss of a loved one through death or divorce, loss of a job, loss of an opportunity, and a loss of something that the individual valued in his/her life. In the case of my Mom, the diagnosis of cancer caused a sense of loss—a loss of a fuller and longer life. In the case of the young woman who experienced divorce, the separation/divorce caused a sense of loss—a loss of perception of a full, successful, and enjoyable married life.

When grief comes, "there is a sense of shock. 'I can't go on. I can't believe it.' Then there's a sense of emotional relief when maybe tears or laughter or another kind of emotional expression breaks through. Then there is the third stage when people begin to feel terribly depressed, isolated, cut off. Sometimes physical symptoms move in. ... Then the fourth stage is a sense of guilt." Some may utter, "If I had only done this" or "If I had only done that, then this would not have happened." "The fifth stage is a sense of anger ... In anger, you reach out and fight at the world for what's happened to you. The last stage is a sense of hope where the cloud breaks and hope emerges."[3] At this stage, one can begin to understand the Apostle Paul's statement, *"Grieve, but not as men who have no hope."* (1 Thessalonians 4:13). In ministry we can and should minister at each stage of grief—allowing the individual to express their shock, their brief emotional relief, their sense of depression, their sense of being stranded or cut off, their anger, and ultimately their sense of hope. The individual should not be rushed through this process, but should be given an opportunity to work through each stage of grief at his/her own pace. As ministers, we need to be sensitive to the needs of the individual and show the compassion that one needs as he/she experiences these stages. We need to help them work through the grief and guide them to the final stage of "hope."

In our world, today, people often believe that one should hide their emotions—do not cry or do not grieve. This notion is unscriptural. The prophet Jeremiah wept over a nation, Israel. He cried out and grieved for the nation. In the crying out, "God moved in and gave him a sense of hope."[4] The prophet Isaiah wept over the Israelites. After he had emptied himself in sorrow and grief, he was able to say, *"Surely He hath borne our grief, and carried our sorrows ..."* (Isaiah 53:4). Thus, as ministers we should not be in a hurry to rush the parishioner through his/her grief. We should walk with them through their suffering and their grief. We should be to them a listening post and a place of support to help them through their difficult times. We should encourage them to cry out unto their God for strength and for help in bearing their grief. We should remind them of the words of the prophet Isaiah, "... *He hath borne our grief, and carried our sorrows,*" that God is with each of us to bear our grief and to carry our sorrows. We are not alone. We are not stranded. We have divine help during difficult times.

We need to develop creative ways to help our parishioners through this process. We must consider designing creative ways that can be unique to each individual within the community. The means for aiding parishioners through this is the use of creativity and play. We might consider getting started in this process by allowing the individual to write down or journal their experiences. Journaling helps the individual to work through their own story—their own periods of grief, despair, and suffering. In the storytelling, which is creativity, one can work through life's difficulties by writing their own stories. Through the writing, one may discover or re-discover that they are not alone in their difficulties—that family and friends, ministers, and colleagues are on hand to support them through their difficult times. Also, one may re-discover that God is with him/her bearing the grief and sorrows with them and leading them to that place of hope.

Through creativity and play, my Mom was able to cope with the ravages of cancer by becoming involved in new things. She began to take voice lessons. (This is something that I did not know that Mom ever had a desire to do. Thusly, I got to learn a little bit more about my Mom.) She really enjoyed these lessons and began to sing with the church choir. She was at play with God. She was in the "flow" as described above. She had identified a clear goal—to take voice lessons. She received immediate feedback. She was accepted among the vocalist and by the voice instructor. She experienced balance between the challenges and skills, which resulted in an "enjoyable game" for her. During this activity of play, distractions were excluded and time seemed to become shortened. For her, music became "auto telic"—an end in itself. There was no other reason for engaging in this other than for "the experience (it) provide(s)—the joy of the experience. Her singing and ministering in song to the Lord brought her great joy and spiritual uplift, in spite of the circumstances of cancer.[5]

Healing Brokenness Through Creativity and Play

In addition to this Mom began to travel more. She traveled with the "Swinging Seniors"—a group of seniors within her church parish, who believed in enjoying life, having fun, and doing new and exciting things together, especially traveling. Mom traveled extensively with this group. In fact, one month prior to her death she was in Canada with this group. Again, she was in the flow. I can remember her words shortly after this trip, "Tomorrow isn't promised to us." She said this to say that each of us should make the most of each day—to enjoy the time at hand, because from her perspective, one never knows when it may come to an end. I learned that she was saying further that we should enjoy the life that God has given to us, even in the midst of suffering and even in the midst of brokenness. When we learn to enjoy the blessings of life, at hand, we are given an opportunity to be creative and we can play in spite of suffering and brokenness.

In her final days, Mom appeared to be extremely content. She had learned how to flow. She was probably the most content person that I have ever known, who has had great difficulties in her life with which to deal. In spite of the difficulties, she had lived her life to the fullest. She had prayed for the deliverance of an alcoholic husband, who was miraculously delivered and had remained sober for over twenty years, without the aid of a 12-Step program, but through intercessory prayer and the miracle of God. She had raised two daughters, who are successful in their own right. She had influenced the development of her granddaughters, who were nurtured by her. She had served as the matriarch of the family and continued to provide wisdom to the family (near and far) throughout her life. Further, she had been creative and played in the final stages of her life. She was content in her creativity and her play—in her singing and her travels—her life (her accomplishments). She was content with her God. Through creativity and play, she was able to cope with the ravages of cancer and she was able to be strengthened and receive spiritual and emotional healing and wholeness.

To experience healing and wholeness, William Self suggests a number of creative things that he considers as a part of the "Survival Kit." These include, for example, when feeling guilty about something, imagining Jesus holding you in His arms and saying, "I love you. You are still My child even though you disobeyed Me. I still love you and you're still My child."[6] At times of fear, remember that "Jesus is with you." Jesus said that He would never leave nor forsake you, not even at death, because He has already conquered death. At times of illness, Self suggests that we remember His apostle, Paul, who requested that the "thorn in the flesh" be removed. He asked three times and the Lord revealed to Paul that His grace (power and unmerited favor) was "sufficient" for Paul. Sufficient is translated in the Greek as "more than enough." God goes on to say to Paul that God's *power is made perfect in weakness*" (2 Corinthians 12:9). We are reminded that God's grace is more than enough for us and during our weakest moments, God's power is at work within us. Self goes on to say that we should "take the best medical advice available" and "wait and see what" God does "in the midst of" the illness. God is still in the healing business. The healing may not mean a cure. It may mean a healing of the spirit and/or of the soul— the mind, will, and emotions. God heals those areas that need God's healing touch.[7] When one feels alone, Self suggests that we remember that God loves us and that it is OK to "cry to God, in Jesus' name, to help you bear your pain." He goes on to say that we should talk out our concerns to God. In addition, we should remember our "life-support systems: people and family, work and projects. ... gracefully reach out to" others. The aid of others helps us until divine help comes.[8] Some of the ways in which God reveals God's love to us is "through His church, our family of faith."[9] So in times of feelings of despair, we should remember that God continues to be with us and often in the presence of family, friends, and colleagues. "A true friend is a real treasure."[10] During difficult times, we discover who true friends really are—those who reflect the love, comfort, and compassion of God. As ministers, we learn to be a "true friend" to those we serve.

Self concludes his Survival Kit by noting that the best way to survive is to have "true faith," an in-depth love and trust of God. In addition, we are to have "true grit"—allows you to "accept yourself as you are and understand ... that every stage of life brings a new kind of insight."[11] True grit means just digging in, facing life, "knowing that

God has promised to bring us through even the difficulties of life."[12] Regardless of what life brings, we are reminded by David in the Scriptures, *"Yea, though I walk through the valley of the shadow of death, I will fear no evil, for thou art with me..."* (Psalm 23:4). God is with us, even through the difficult times. True faith and true grit give us the fortitude to hold onto the promises of God that have been set forth in the Scriptures. True faith and true grit may also provide the soul strength that allows us to play our way through critical junctures in our lives. Scriptural promises sustain us and sustain those to whom and with whom we minister.

Chapter 5

Conclusion

In conclusion, ministers should find ways to aid those who are dealing with suffering and feelings of brokenness. We are reminded that each person "could be made more creative."[1] Thereby causing "our days (to be) filled with wonder and excitement."[2] Mom was continuing to fill her days with wonder and excitement. She had learned to "make time for ... relaxation" and enjoyment.[3] She had decided to "start doing more of what" she loved.[4] She had thought through her heart's desire and began to implement those desires. She had chosen new domains for herself—music and travel. She was accepted and encouraged by the peers within the domains. Her experiences within the domains had done "wonders for the quality of" her life.⁵ Csikszentmihalyi tells us that "what really matters, in the last account, is ... whether you have lived a full and creative life." Surely Mom did.

The young woman, who was affected by abuse in her marriage, is working through her brokenness through being creative. She has chosen to pour herself into researching and writing her dissertation in Electrical Engineering. As a graduate with a Masters Degree in Electrical Engineering from Stanford University, this young woman has been accepted among her colleagues within the domain—Electrical Engineering. Her peers and her superiors within the field of "Systems on a Chip" recognize her as a talented, gifted, and creative individual within the field. She, too, has learned how to experience "the flow" of her creativity. She has learned to play by being creative in her work and benefiting from each of the nine elements of being in the flow, including immediate feedback; her "abilities are well-matched to the opportunities for action." She is no longer distracted by spousal issues and is focused on the challenges and skills of completing the tasks at hand regarding the thesis. For her these experiences have become auto telic—become an "end in itself." For her, the research and discoveries of the new are exciting and affirming.[6] She has found "healing and wholeness" in being creative within her field. In spite of the difficulties of marital problems, separation, brokenness, and divorce, she has learned that by being creative, she is being made whole—experiencing healing and wholeness spiritually, emotionally, and even physically. She has told me recently that she "feels at peace." She is experiencing peace in her home, peace on the job, and peace overall in her life.

She has stated that the peace has come about by spending time in prayer, lying prostrate before God, by crying out to God in her despair, by sensing God's Presence—the "hope" of God that her life is getting better. She has said that she has been "delivered from depression" and she has much more joy and happiness in her life. She has discovered that "what really matters, in the last account," is to live a full and creative life. Her work life and her academic life are aiding in this process. She has learned to be creative and experience play—fun in what she is developing. This new focus, together with God, who is our burden bearer, is helping this young

Healing Brokenness Through Creativity and Play

woman to experience healing and wholeness. She has learned what really matters—to live life to the fullest through creativity and play.[7]

These are the tasks for the ministers as we minister unto God's creation, to aid in ministering healing and wholeness through creativity and play. In providing Pastoral Care, we need to use our compassion and empathy. We need to be good and active listeners. We need to ask probative questions to get at the heart of what is troubling the individual. We need to guide the individual through the stages of grief, their sense of loss, to the point of hope. We need to help to re-direct their thought processes through areas of creativity and play: through the telling of their own stories (or journaling), through doing something that perhaps they have always wanted to do (like taking vocal lessons), and through being creative within their domain and field, for example in the field of Electrical Engineering—creating new systems on a chip. These are some of the ways in which ministers can aid the parishioner in reaching healing and wholeness through creativity and play.

Conclusion

As ministers, we are called to minister to God's creation by acting as messengers of God's Word, servants of God—revealing God's love, mercy, and grace, and helpers to aid the divine revelation and divine vision to become "actualized as shalom"—peace—in the lives of children, adolescents, adults, and seniors.[8] We are called to aid humanity through the struggles of life. We are called to create and help them to create *"beauty for ashes"* (Isaiah 61:3).

End Notes

Chapter 2

1. James Strong, The New Strong's Exhaustive Concordance of the Bible, (New York: Thomas Nelson Publishers, 1984), Hebrew and Chaldee Dictionary, 107.)

2. Ibid, 54.

3. Ibid, 31.

4. Webster's Ninth New Collegiate Dictionary (Springfield: A Merriam-Webster Inc., 1988), 1098.

Chapter 3

1. Mihaly Csikszentmihalyi, Creativity, (New York: Harper-Perennial: 1996), vii

2. Ibid, 1.

3. Ibid.

4. Ibid, 6.

5. Ibid, 8.

6. Ibid, 27.
7. Ibid, 28.
8. Ibid.
9. Ibid.
10. Ibid.
11. Ibid.
12. Ibid, 308.
13. Ibid, 310.
14. Ibid, 309.
15. Daniel Goleman, Emotional Intelligence, (New York: Bantam Books, 1997), xii.
16. Ibid, xix.
17. Ibid, 83.
18. Ibid, 84
19. Ibid, 87.
20. Ibid.
21. Ibid.
22. Ibid, 88.
23. Ibid, 151.
24. Ibid.
25. Ibid, 154.

26. Ibid.

27. Ibid.

28. Ibid, 268.

29. Ibid.

30. Ibid.

31. Catherine Garvey, Play, (Cambridge: Harvard University, United Press, 1977), 2.

32. Ibid, 3.

33. Ibid.

34. Ibid.

35. Ibid.

36. Ibid.

37. Ibid, 5.

38. Ibid, 82

39. Ibid, 96.

40. R. Herron and B. Sutton-Smith, eds., Child's Play (New York: Wiley, 1971)

41. Garvey, 97.

42. Michael S. Koppel, "A Pastoral Theological Reflection on Play in the Ministry," Journal of Pastoral Theology, Vol. 13, No. 1, Spring 2003.

43. Ibid.

44. Ibid.

45. Ibid.

46. Ibid.

47. Ibid.

48. Ibid and D. W. Winnicott, Playing and Reality. (New York: Basic Books, 1971), 53.

49. Ibid.

Chapter 4

1. William L. Self and Carolyn Self, Survival Kit for the Stranded, (Nashville: Broadman Press, 1975), 16.

2. Ibid

3. Ibid, 17.

4. Ibid, 19.

5. Mihaly Csikszentmihalyi, Creativity, (New York: Harper-Perennial, 1996), 110-113.

6. William Self, 32.

7. Ibid, 52.

8. Ibid, 80.

9. Ibid, 87.

10. Ibid, 141.

11. Ibid, 133-137.

12. Ibid, 138.

Chapter 5

1. Csikszentmihalyi, 343.

2. Ibid.

3. Ibid, 353.

4. Ibid, 357.

5. Ibid, 371.

6. Ibid, 111-113.

7. Ibid.

8. Gordon E. Jackson, Creating Something of Beauty, (St. Louis: Chalice Press, 1998), 115.

Bibliography

Csikszentmihalyi, Mihaly. *Creativity*. New York: Harper-Perennial, 1996.

Garvey, Catherine. *Play*. Cambridge: Harvard University United Press, 1997.

Goleman, Daniel. *Emotional Intelligence*. New York: Bantam Books, 1997.

Herron, R. and B. Sutton-Smith, eds. *Child's Play*. New York: Wiley, 1971.

Jackson, Gordon E. Creating Something of Beauty. St. Louis: Chalice Press, 1998.

Koppel, Michael S. "A Pastoral Theological Reflection on Play in the Ministry." *Journal of Pastoral Theology*. Volume 13, Number 1, Spring 2003.

Self, William L. and Carolyn Self. *Survival Kit for the Stranded*. Nashville: Broadman Press, 1975.

Strong, James. *The New Strong's Exhaustive Concordance of the Bible*. New York: Thomas Nelson Publishers, 1984.

The Comparative Study Bible. Grand Rapids: The Zondervan Bible Publishers, 1984.

Webster's Ninth New Collegiate Dictionary. Springfield: Merriam-Webster Inc., 1988.

Winnicott, D.W. *Playing and Reality*. New York: Basic Books, 1971.

About the Author

Dr. Carolyn V. Hodge is a native of the Nation's Capital. Formerly, she was the Director of Equal Employment Opportunity with the Department of Justice, Immigration and Naturalization Service. With a plethora of ministry experience, Dr. Hodge has served as Pulpit Minister; as Associate Pastor; as Assistant Pastor; and currently as Founder and Pastor of "I AM The Living Word Ministries."

Dr. Hodge completed graduate study at Antioch School of Law earning a Master's degree in Equal Opportunity Law. She earned a Master of Divinity degree (receiving the Dean's Top Graduate Award) from Howard University School of Divinity (HUSD). As a result of this exposure, she served as Assistant Chaplain at the National Rehabilitation Hospital in Washington, D.C. She received an Honorary Doctor of Divinity degree; and earned a Doctor of Ministry degree from Wesley Theological Seminary of Washington, D.C. Dr. Hodge was ordained a Reverend in the Pentecostal Discipline and licensed in the D.C. Superior Court in 1999 under the leadership of Rev. Dr. Judy Fisher, Senior Pastor of the Church of the Lords Missions International of Washington, D.C.

www.ingramcontent.com/pod-product-compliance
Lightning Source LLC
Chambersburg PA
CBHW072108290426
44110CB00014B/1873